party &
snack
perfection

HINKLER
BOOKS

party &
snack
perfection

Food Editor
Jody Vassallo

Creative Director
Sam Grimmer

Project Editor
Lara Morcombe

HB
HINKLER
BOOKS

First published in 2004 by Hinkler Books Pty Ltd
45–55 Fairchild Street
Heatherton Victoria Australia 3202
www.hinklerbooks.com

10 9 8 7

10 09 08

ISBN: 978-1-8651-5770-2

Printed and bound in China

contents

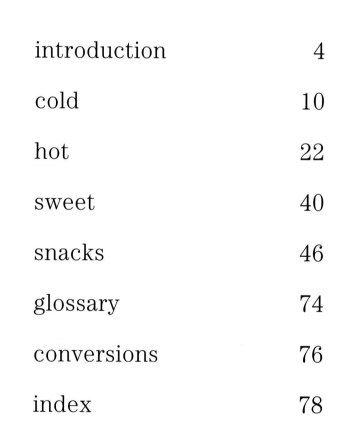

an introduction to party and snack perfection

Whether it's to celebrate a birthday, a new house, a new year or just to gather together a group of friends and acquaintances, parties can be a source of such pleasure. Inherent in the pleasure of a party is the food. Imagine platters of lobster filo triangles circulating guests in tandem with Morrocan lemon shish kebabs or prune and prosciutto rolls. This book offers exciting finger food recipes to suit every taste and every occasion.

organisation

Long before the event, parties require considerable organisation. Decisions need to be made about venues, numbers, decorations, themes, invitations and, of course, food and drink. Planning your menu well ahead will minimise unexpected last minute headaches. Think about what types of food, quantities, cooking practicalities and serving utensils.

Firstly, do not rule out buying a few pre-made party foods such as baby gourmet pies, satay sticks, spring rolls and Asian dumplings. They can be well priced, good quality and readily available.

When you plan the menu, consider the size of your oven. If you plan too many hot dishes, you may have trouble finding oven space and the time to heat them all. It's also best if you cook things beforehand and only use the oven to warm things before serving. If you have frozen foods, defrost them in advance. It is also a good idea to serve cold dishes such as dips and crudités, antipasto platters and cheese plates as these do not require much preparation and can be made well ahead of time.

You will need plenty of platters. If it's a big party, you may need to hire some from a party hire store. You may also need to hire other things such as glasses, and tables and chairs. Napkins should be placed onto each platter so guests can take a napkin with the food. Cocktail sticks or toothpicks might also be needed if you are serving meatballs. Place a few bins around the room for things such as bones or olive seeds.

Finally, if it is a large party you may want to consider employing waiting staff to assist you. Hospitality agencies have experienced people who can help make your job easier. They can hand around food, top up guests' drinks and clean up the aftermath, giving you time to relax and enjoy the party.

timing

Timing is important. Dips and antipasto platters or cheese plates can be put out for when people arrive, allowing you time to greet your guests and fill their glasses. Once everyone has arrived you can begin warming and serving the food. It is often a good idea to alternate meat-based bites with vegetarian bites. Finally, unless your gathering is an afternoon tea or garden party, serve the sweet food last.

presentation

A little effort with presentation goes a long way. Decorating a platter with edible flowers such as nasturtiums can brighten up the whole room. Adding a small herb sprig to canapés will add extra colour. Serving bite-size treats on Chinese spoons or in a bamboo steamer will create an Asian vibe. Lining platters with paper doilies or banana leaves will stop food from sliding across the platter as you walk around the room.

how much to serve?

Not having enough food is every host's nightmare, and as a result most people tend to over cater. The following is a rough guide to quantities:

pre-dinner nibbles
allow 3–5 pieces per person

for a 2–3 hour cocktail party
allow 4–6 pieces per person

for a party with no main meal
allow 8–12 pieces per person

As a general rule, for up to 20 people you should plan 6 different dishes. For more than 20 people, you should consider 8–10 dishes.

for drinks
For a 2–3 hour cocktail party allow 1 bottle of wine between 2 people. White is usually more popular than red. If serving champagne, allow 3 glasses per person.

Always have soda, mineral water and soft drinks on hand. Buy plenty of ice and have lots of glasses – usually 2–3 per person depending on the occasion. If people are drinking beer and wine, attach a few bottle openers to a spot near where the drinks are being served.

invitations

Invitations can be used to inform people about what to expect. For instance, you can make it clear that you will be serving finger food, so that people do not arrive expecting a sit down meal. Invites can also help with planning food. If you have any guests with special dietary requirements such as vegetarianism, remind them to let you know about it when they RSVP. Finally, don't forget to specify whether alcohol is provided or not.

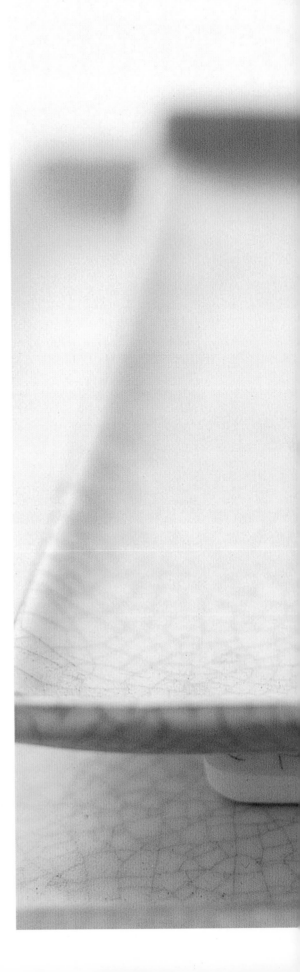

cold

blinis with herbed yoghurt cheese

ingredients

1 teaspoon dry yeast
1 teaspoon sugar
1¹/₂ cups (375 ml, 12 fl oz) milk, warmed
125 g (4 oz) buckwheat flour
125 g (4 oz) plain flour
1 egg white
freshly ground black pepper
cooking oil spray
¹/₂ cup (125 g, 4 oz) greek-style yoghurt
1 tablespoon chopped fresh dill
1 tablespoon chopped fresh mint
semi-dried tomatoes for garnish
  (optional)
makes 20

i

preparation time
15 minutes

cooking time
20-25 minutes

nutritional value per serve
fat: 20.8 g
carbohydrate: 21.9 g
protein: 5.2 g

1 In a small bowl, place yeast, sugar and ¹/₂ cup (125 ml, 4 fl oz) milk. Stand for 5 minutes or until frothy.

2 In a large bowl, place buckwheat flour and plain flour. Mix to combine. Make a well in the centre and pour yeast mixture and remaining milk into well. Mix until just combined.

3 Place egg white in a separate clean bowl. Beat until soft peaks form. Fold egg mixture into batter. Season with black pepper to taste.

4 Heat a large nonstick frying pan over a medium heat. Lightly spray with cooking oil. Place tablespoons of mixture in pan and cook in batches for 12 minutes or until bubbles appear on the surface. Turn and cook second side for 30 seconds or until golden. Place on kitchen paper and keep warm. In a small bowl, place yoghurt, dill and mint, and mix well to combine.

5 Serve blinis warm or cold topped with a spoonful of yoghurt mixture and semi-dried tomatoes if desired.

salami stacks

ingredients

250 g (8 oz) cream cheese
90 g (3 oz) diced dried apricots
4 tablespoons mayonnaise
$^1/_2$ teaspoon tabasco sauce
16 slices danish salami
extra 135 g (4$^3/_4$ oz) diced apricots,
    very finely chopped
makes 24

1 Bring cream cheese to room temperature, cream well, using a wooden spoon, to soften. Reserve 3 tablespoons cream cheese, leave at room temperature. Stir 90 g (3 oz) diced apricots, mayonnaise and tabasco into cream cheese.

2 Lay 4 salami slices on a clean board. Spread a heaped teaspoon of cheese mixture on each slice, making sure it is spread right to the edge. Place second salami slice on top and spread as above. Repeat with one more slice

and top with the fourth slice. Place on a flat plate, cover with plastic wrap and refrigerate for 2 hours.

3 Take the extra 135 g (4$^3/_4$ oz) of very finely chopped apricots. Spread on kitchen paper in a 1$^1/_2$ cm-wide strip.

Lightly spread reserved cream cheese around the sides of the salami stacks. Roll the sides of the stacks over the chopped apricots, press on well. Cover and refrigerate. To serve, cut each stack into 6 triangles. Place a toothpick in centre of each and arrange on platter.

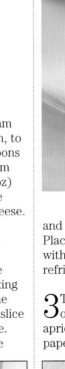

preparation time
15 minutes,
plus 2 hours
refrigeration

cooking time
20 minutes

**nutritional value
per serve**
fat: 25 g
carbohydrate: 13.6 g
protein: 12 g

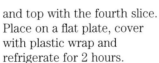

olive scones with thyme cured beef

ingredients

chutney of your choice
fresh thyme sprigs
thyme cured beef
185 g (6 oz) sugar
125 g (4 oz) salt
3 tablespoons crushed black peppercorns
1 large bunch (about 60 g, 2 oz) fresh
   thyme, leaves only
200 g (7 oz) lean beef fillet, trimmed
   of visible fat
olive scones
oil for greasing
250 g (8 oz) plain flour
2 teaspoons baking powder
45 g (1½ oz) black olives, chopped
1 tablespoon chopped fresh basil
freshly ground black pepper
1 cup (250 ml, 8 fl oz) buttermilk
1 tablespoon dijon mustard
makes 24 scones or 48 open-faced canapés

i

preparation time
20 minutes, plus
24 hour
refrigeration

cooking time
20 minutes

nutritional value
fat: 3.3 g
carbohydrate: 30.1 g
protein: 5.1 g

2 Using absorbent kitchen paper, thoroughly wipe away the herb crust. Using a sharp knife, cut beef across the grain into paper-thin slices – this is easier if you place the fillet in the freezer for 10 minutes before slicing. Place slices on a plate, cover and refrigerate until ready to use.

3 For the scones: Preheat oven to 200°C (400°F, gas mark 6). Lightly brush a baking tray with oil and set aside.

4 Into a large bowl, sift flour and baking powder. Add olives, basil and black pepper to taste. Mix to combine. Make a well in the centre. In a small bowl, place milk and mustard. Whisk to combine and pour into flour mixture. Mix quickly to make a soft dough. Turn dough onto a lightly floured surface. Knead lightly until smooth.

5 Press dough or roll out to form a 2 cm thick rectangle. Using a 3 cm scone cutter, cut out scones. Place with sides just touching on prepared baking tray. Bake for 10–12 minutes or until scones are well risen and golden. Transfer to a wire rack. Cool slightly.

6 To serve, split scones and spread with a little chutney. Top with a small mound of beef and a thyme sprig.

1 To cure beef: Place sugar, salt, peppercorns and thyme leaves on a large plate. Roll beef in mixture several times to coat and form a crust. Place beef on a wire rack set in a shallow dish. Cover and refrigerate for 24 hours, checking occasionally that the crust remains intact.

gravlax spirals

ingredients

125 g (4 oz) ricotta cheese
3 tablespoons chopped fresh dill
$^{1}/_{2}$ cup (125 g, 4 oz) natural yoghurt
2 slices lavash bread
4 tablespoons honey mustard
100 g (3$^{1}/_{2}$ oz) gravlax, smoked salmon
  or smoked ocean trout
lemon juice
freshly ground black pepper
makes 20

i

preparation time
15 minutes,
plus 2 hours
refrigeration

cooking time
10 minutes

**nutritional value
per serve**
fat: 3.8 g
carbohydrate: 6.6 g
protein: 8 g

1 In large bowl, place ricotta cheese, dill and yoghurt. Mix well to combine and set aside.

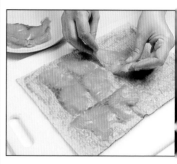

2 Spread lavash bread with mustard. Top with salmon. Spread with ricotta mixture, leaving 10 cm at one short end uncovered. Drizzle with lemon juice and black pepper to taste.

3 Starting at the covered short end, roll up firmly. Wrap in plastic food wrap. Refrigerate for 2 hours or until ready to serve.

4 To serve, cut rolls into 2 cm thick slices. Arrange on a serving platter.

oysters bloody mary

1 In a bowl, combine vodka, tabasco, pepper, lime juice, tomato flesh and mustard.

2 Spread mixture evenly over opened oysters and grill under a pre-heated grill for

5–10 minutes, or serve chilled. Serve with crusty bread or toast and garnish with lime wedges.

i

preparation time
5 minutes

cooking time
5-10 minutes

nutritional value per serve
fat: 0.5 g
carbohydrate: 1.6 g
protein: 2.7 g

ingredients

1 tablespoon vodka
1 dash tabasco
freshly ground black pepper
squeeze of fresh lime
flesh of 2 fresh tomatoes, chopped (no pulp or seeds)
$^1/_2$-1 teaspoon whole-grain mustard (optional)
6 scrubbed oysters, shucked
lime wedges to serve
makes 6

apricot canapés

ingredients

250 g (8 oz) cream cheese
1/2 cup (125 ml, 4 fl oz) mayonnaise
60 g (2 oz) chopped walnuts
2 teaspoons sherry (optional)
200 g (7 oz) large dried apricots
makes 25–30

preparation time
10 minutes

nutritional value per serve
fat: 25.3 g
carbohydrate: 18.7 g
protein: 6.1 g

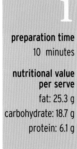

1 In a large bowl, combine cream cheese and mayonnaise and mix until soft and fluffy. Add walnuts and sherry, and mix to combine.

2 Place a teaspoon of mixture onto each dried apricot and arrange on a platter. Serve at room temperature.

ham and cheese savouries

preparation time
10 minutes, plus
1 hour
refrigeration

nutritional value per serve
fat: 11.3 g
carbohydrate: 33 g
protein: 9.5 g

ingredients

250 g (8 oz) cream cheese
1/2 cup (125 g, 4 oz) plain yoghurt
140 g (4 1/2 oz) diced dried apricots
2 tablespoons chopped seeded raisins
200 g (7 oz) shaved ham, finely chopped
1 packet water crackers
makes 25–30

1 In a large bowl, mix cream cheese until softened. Stir in yoghurt. Mix until combined. In a separate bowl, combine apricots, raisins and ham, mix evenly, then stir into cream cheese mixture. Refrigerate for 1 hour.

2 Heap a tablespoon of mixture onto each cracker and serve.

brandied prune pinwheels

ingredients

8 large prunes
1 tablespoon brandy
100 g (3½ oz) ricotta cheese
1 teaspoon ground cinnamon
8 slices square-cut chicken loaf or
  thinly-sliced sandwich ham

makes 35

1 Remove pit from prunes, then finely dice. Work knife back and forth until prunes are almost pulverised. Place in a bowl and add the brandy. Stand 10 minutes.

2 Add ricotta cheese and cinnamon to the prunes. Spread a heaped teaspoonful onto the chicken loaf or ham slices, spreading right to the edges. Roll up and place,

seam side down, on a plate, cover and refrigerate 1 hour. Cut into 4–5 pieces and serve, cut side up, to show pinwheel effect.

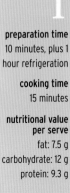

preparation time
10 minutes, plus 1
hour refrigeration

cooking time
15 minutes

**nutritional value
per serve**
fat: 7.5 g
carbohydrate: 12 g
protein: 9.3 g

prune and proscuitto rolls

ingredients

150 g (5 oz) proscuitto
250 g (8 oz) pitted prunes
toothpicks
makes 24

i

preparation time
5 minutes

**nutritional value
per serve**
fat: 2.2 g
carbohydrate: 27.5 g
protein: 8.2 g

1 Cut each proscuitto slice in half across the width and then in half again down its length.

2 Wrap a strip of proscuitto around each prune. Secure with a toothpick. Serve as an hors d'oeuvre.

eggplant dip

ingredients

1 large eggplant (aubergine)
1 tablespoon lemon juice
2 medium tomatoes
1 medium onion, chopped
2 cloves garlic, crushed
3 tablespoons olive oil
$\frac{1}{2}$ teaspoon salt
$\frac{1}{2}$ teaspoon lemon pepper
$\frac{1}{8}$ teaspoon freshly ground black
    pepper
1 packet water crackers or toasted
    turkish bread
makes about 750 g (1$\frac{1}{2}$ lb)

i

preparation time
15 minutes

cooking time
30-35 minutes

**nutritional value
per serve**
fat: 5.7 g
carbohydrate: 27.2 g
protein: 4.7 g

1 To create the eggplant serving dish: Place the eggplant on its side and determine which side will serve as the base. Cut off the top side in a shallow slice and hollow out the flesh leaving a 5–10 mm shell. Rub the edge of the shell with lemon juice, wrap it tightly and refrigerate.

2 Chop the eggplant flesh coarsely. Peel, seed and coarsely chop the tomatoes.

3 Heat olive oil in a large frying pan and sauté the eggplant, tomatoes, onion and garlic on a medium-high heat for 5–6 minutes. Reduce heat, add the salt, lemon pepper and black pepper and simmer for 20–25 minutes. Remove the frying pan from heat and allow to cool to room temperature.

4 Place mixture in a food processor and process until combined. Refrigerate until needed.

5 When ready to serve fill the reserved eggplant shell with dip and garnish with parsley. Serve with water crackers or toasted turkish bread.

hot

mini pizzas

ingredients

1 teaspoon active dry yeast
pinch sugar
$2/3$ cup (170 ml, $5^1/2$ fl oz) warm water
250 g (8 oz) plain flour
$1/2$ teaspoon salt
4 tablespoons olive oil

classic pizza topping

185 g (6 oz) tomato paste
dried oregano leaves
315 g (10 oz) cherry tomatoes, sliced
125 g (4 oz) pepperoni or cabanossi,
  thinly sliced
20-25 pitted black olives, thinly sliced
250 g (8 oz) mozzarella cheese, grated

makes about 80

3 Place dough in a lightly oiled bowl and roll around bowl to cover surface with oil. Cover bowl with plastic food wrap and place in a warm, draught-free place for 1–1$1/2$ hours or until doubled in size. Knock down and knead lightly.

1 To make dough: In a small bowl, place yeast, sugar and water and mix to dissolve. Set aside in a warm place for 5 minutes or until mixture is foamy.

2 Place flour and salt in a food processor and pulse until combined. With machine running, slowly pour in yeast mixture and oil and process to make a rough dough. Turn dough onto a lightly floured surface and knead for 5 minutes or until soft and shiny. Add more flour if necessary.

4 Preheat oven to 190°C (375°F, gas mark 5). Divide dough into 4 cm balls, press out to make 7 cm circles and place on greased baking trays. Spread each dough circle with tomato paste, then sprinkle with oregano and top with slices of tomato, pepperoni or cabanossi and olives. Sprinkle with cheese and bake at 190°C (375°F, gas mark 5) for 10 minutes or until pizzas are crisp and brown.

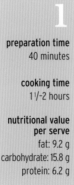

i

preparation time
40 minutes

cooking time
1 $1/$-2 hours

**nutritional value
per serve**
fat: 9.2 g
carbohydrate: 15.8 g
protein: 6.2 g

muffin break

ingredients

4 english muffins, split
200 g (7 oz) shaved ham
4 slices canned pineapple
4 slices tasty cheese
canola oil spray
serves 4

i

preparation time
5 minutes

cooking time
5 minutes

**nutritional value
per serve**
fat: 10.1 g
carbohydrate: 14.9 g
protein: 10.5 g

1 Divide the ham and place on bottom half of each muffin. Top with pineapple slice, cheese slice and close with muffin top.

2 Preheat sandwich press, spray base plate lightly with vegetable oil. Place on the muffins and quickly spray the tops. Close lid and cook for 2–3 minutes or until the cheese has melted sufficiently.

samosas

ingredients

1 tablespoon vegetable oil
2 medium onions, finely chopped
1 clove garlic, crushed
2 teaspoons curry paste
$^1/_2$ teaspoon salt
1 tablespoon white vinegar
250 g (8 oz) chicken mince
$^1/_2$ cup (125 ml, 4 fl oz) water
2 teaspoons sweet chilli sauce
2 tablespoons chopped coriander
1 packet large spring roll wrappers
$1^1/_2$ cups (375 ml, 12 fl oz) vegetable oil

makes 30–36

1 Heat the wok to a medium-high heat. Add oil and fry onions and garlic until softened. Add curry paste and salt and stir to combine. Stir in vinegar. Add chicken mince for 3–4 minutes breaking up mince with the back of a spoon. Reduce heat, add water, cover and cook about 6 minutes until most of the water is absorbed. Add chilli sauce and coriander. Stir until the water has evaporated and mince is dry. Remove to a plate to cool. Rinse wok.

2 Cut 10 spring roll wrappers into 3 even strips. Place a teaspoon of filling at bottom end and fold over the pastry diagonally, forming a triangle. Fold again on the straight; continue to make 3 more folds in same manner. Moisten the inside edge of the last fold with water and press gently to seal.

3 Heat the clean wok. Add enough oil to be approximately 5 cm deep. Heat oil but take care not to overheat. Add 3 or 4 samosas and fry about 3–4 minutes until golden. Remove with a slotted spoon to a tray lined with paper towels. Repeat with remainder. If samosas become dark in colour, immediately remove from heat to drop the oil temperature.

i

preparation time
15 minutes
cooking time
30-40 minutes
nutritional value per serve
fat: 30.9 g
carbohydrate: 10.2 g
protein: 5.6 g

spring rolls

ingredients

2 tablespoons oil
2 teaspoons finely chopped
   fresh ginger
1 small onion, finely chopped
500 g (1 lb) chicken stir-fry pieces,
   finely chopped
$\frac{1}{2}$ chinese cabbage, finely chopped
$\frac{1}{2}$ red capsicum (pepper), seeded
   and thinly sliced
4 mushrooms, thinly sliced
2 teaspoons cornflour
1 tablespoon water
1 tablespoon soy sauce
1 packet large spring roll wrappers
oil for deep frying
dipping sauce
125 g (4 oz) apricot jam
1 tablespoon lemon juice
2 tablespoons white vinegar
1 tablespoon soy sauce
1 tablespoon water
makes 32

1 In a frying pan, place apricot jam, lemon juice, white vinegar, 1 tablespoon soy sauce and 1 tablespoon water. Mix all ingredients together, and heat gently while stirring. Set aside.

2 In the wok add 2 tablespoons oil and heat. Add ginger and onion and stir-fry until onion is pale gold in colour. Add chicken and stir-fry about 2 minutes until white. Toss in cabbage, capsicum and mushrooms and stir-fry for 1 minute, mixing chicken through the vegetables. In a small bowl, combine cornflour and water.

3 Add soy sauce and 2 tablespoons of dipping sauce to the wok, tossing to mix through. Push the ingredients to one side of the wok and add blended cornflour to the juices in the base of the wok. As juices thicken, stir and toss through the vegetables. Remove from heat and spread mixture out onto a flat tray to cool. Wrap 1 heaped tablespoon chicken mixture in each wrapper according to packet directions.

i

preparation time
10 minutes

cooking time
20 minutes

**nutritional value
per serve**
fat: 13.7 g
carbohydrate: 15.7 g
protein: 8.6 g

4 Wipe out the wok, heat and add fresh oil to approximately 5 cm deep. Heat oil and fry rolls a few at a time until golden and crisp. Drain on absorbent paper. Serve hot with dipping sauce.

Tip: Mini spring rolls are ideal finger food for a crowd. Cut spring roll wrappers in half and use 2 teaspoons spring roll mixture. Place mixture on bottom end of strip and roll once. Fold in side and continue to roll. Seal end with a little egg white. Serve with dipping sauce.

honey and sesame chicken

ingredients

500 g (1 lb) chicken breast fillets,
    cut into 1 cm slices
½ teaspoon sesame oil
½ teaspoon five-spice powder
4 tablespoons peanut oil
2 tablespoons cornflour
3 tablespoons honey
1 tablespoon lemon juice
2 tablespoons sesame seeds
batter
90 g (3 oz) self-raising flour
4 tablespoons cornflour
1¼ cups (315 ml, 10 fl oz) water
1 egg white
serves 6

1 Combine sesame oil and five-spice powder in a large bowl, add chicken and toss to coat. Set aside for 15 minutes.

2 Into a large bowl, sift self-raising flour and 4 tablespoons cornflour. Add water and mix until smooth. In a separate bowl, beat egg white until soft peaks form. Fold gently into flour mixture.

3 Heat peanut oil in a wok or large frying pan. Place the 2 tablespoons cornflour in a bowl. Dip each piece of chicken into the cornflour, shake off excess, dip into batter and immediately into hot oil. Cook in batches and drain on absorbent paper. Empty the wok or pan of oil, wipe clean and add honey and lemon juice and gently heat. Return chicken pieces to the pan and toss to coat. Serve sprinkled with sesame seeds.

i

preparation time
20 minutes

cooking time
25 minutes

**nutritional value
per serve**
fat: 4 g
carbohydrate: 16.6 g
protein: 10.9 g

dim sims

ingredients

100 g (3 1/2 oz) prawns, peeled
4 shallots, cut into 2.5 cm lengths
125 g (4 oz) pork mince
1/8 small cabbage, finely chopped
1 egg
2 tablespoons soy sauce
few drops sesame oil
1/2 teaspoon salt
1 tablespoon cornflour
1 packet won ton wrappers
oil for deep frying
makes about 30

1 In a food processor, place prawns and shallots and process until well combined. Add pork, cabbage, egg, soy sauce, sesame oil, salt and cornflour. Process until well combined.

2 Place a teaspoon of mixture into the centre of each won ton wrapper. Pinch the won ton skin together at the top to form a small package.

3 In a wok, heat 5 cm oil and cook dim sims in batches, about 4–5 minutes until golden and cooked through.

4 Drain on kitchen paper and serve with soy sauce or your favourite dipping sauce.

i

preparation time
25 minutes

cooking time
30 minutes

nutritional value per serve
fat: 25 g
carbohydrate: 7.7 g
protein: 6.4 g

deep-fried crab balls

ingredients

450 g (14 oz) crabmeat, flaked
4 tablespoons butter, softened
1 tablespoon dijon mustard
$1/8$ teaspoon tabasco sauce
2 egg yolks
45 g ($1^1/2$ oz) fresh breadcrumbs
salt
125 g (4 oz) plain flour
$1/2$ cup (125 ml, 4 fl oz) oil
   for deep frying
tartare sauce
250 g (8 oz) egg mayonnaise
1 teaspoon finely grated onion
1 teaspoon finely chopped parsley
1 teaspoon finely chopped basil
1 teaspoon finely chopped gherkins
1 teaspoon finely chopped green olives
1 teaspoon dijon mustard
salt and pepper
makes 36

1 In a large bowl, combine crabmeat, butter, 1 tablespoon mustard, tabasco, egg yolks and breadcrumbs. Mix well, add salt to taste, cover and refrigerate until firm.

2 Shape into balls the size of a small walnut, and refrigerate for a further 30 minutes. Roll in flour and deep fry in hot oil for 4–5 minutes until golden. Drain on paper towels.

i

preparation time
15 minutes,
plus 45 minutes
refrigeration

cooking time
5 minutes

nutritional value per serve
fat: 24.4 g
carbohydrate: 15.8 g
protein: 4.3 g

3 In a small bowl, combine mayonnaise, onion, parsley, basil, gherkins, olives and 1 teaspoon dijon mustard. Refrigerate until required. Serve crab balls dipped in tartare sauce.

fresh salmon rolls

ingredients

500 g (1 lb) piece salmon, skin removed
4 tablespoons seasoned rice vinegar
4 tablespoons lime juice
2 tablespoons chopped fresh coriander
1 teaspoon grated fresh ginger
4 spring onions (green onions)
12 rounds rice paper wrappers
1 carrot, peeled and julienned
extra ¹/₂ bunch fresh coriander
¹/₂ cup (125 ml, 4 fl oz) peanut oil,
  for frying

dipping sauce

1 tablespoon soy sauce
1 tablespoon fish sauce
2 teaspoons sugar
2 tablespoons fresh parsley leaves
¹/₂ bunch fresh coriander
3 tablespoons lime juice
2 tablespoons rice vinegar
2 teaspoons grated fresh ginger

makes 12

1 Cut the salmon fillet into 12 fingers, each about 8 x 2 cm. In a large bowl, whisk 4 tablespoons rice vinegar, 4 tablespoons lime juice, 2 tablespoons coriander and 1 teaspoon ginger. Add the

salmon pieces and marinate for 30 minutes.

2 In a small bowl, whisk together soy sauce, fish sauce, sugar, parsley, ¹/₂ bunch coriander and the remaining lime juice, rice vinegar and ginger. Set sauce aside.

3 Cut spring onions into 8 cm lengths then finely slice into thin strips lengthways. Remove the salmon from marinade and pat dry.

4 Fill a large bowl with warm water and soak the rice paper wrappers, one at a time, until softened. When one wrapper is soft, place it on a clean tea towel and place a

piece of salmon on top. Add strips of spring onion, carrot and some coriander leaves, roll up tightly, folding the sides in as you roll. Place on a large tray, seam down, and repeat method until all the ingredients have been used.

5 In a large frying pan or wok, add peanut oil to a depth of 2 cm and heat. Fry the rolls, seam side down, until golden underneath, then turn and cook the other side, about 3–4 minutes. Drain on absorbent paper and serve immediately with dipping sauce.

i

preparation time
30 minutes, plus 30 minutes marinating

cooking time
8-12 minutes

nutritional value per serve
fat: 11.6 g
carbohydrate: 8.2 g
protein: 8.6 g

scallop puffs

ingredients

250 g (8 oz) sea scallops
4 tablespoons mayonnaise
60 g (2 oz) gruyère, freshly grated
1/2 teaspoon dijon mustard
1 teaspoon fresh lemon juice
1 tablespoon finely chopped fresh
  parsley
salt and pepper
1 large egg white
8 slices crusty white bread, toasted
  lightly, crusts discarded, and each
    slice cut into 4 squares
1 sheet puff pastry, cut into 25 squares
  (each 5 x 5 cm)

makes 32

preparation time
10 minutes

cooking time
20 minutes

nutritional value
fat: 10.3 g
carbohydrate: 22.4 g
protein: 8.7 g

1 Preheat oven to 160°C (315°F, gas mark 2–3). In a large pan combine scallops with enough salted water to cover completely, bring the water to a simmer, and poach scallops for 5 minutes. Drain well and cut into 1 cm pieces.

2 In a large bowl, whisk together mayonnaise, gruyère, mustard, lemon juice, parsley, salt and pepper, add scallops, and toss mixture well. In a small bowl, beat the egg white until it forms stiff peaks. Fold into scallop mixture gently but thoroughly.

3 Prick pastry squares with a fork and place on a lined oven tray. Bake for 5 minutes until lightly golden.

4 Preheat grill to medium high. Remove pastry from oven and place a heaped teaspoon of the scallop mixture onto each. Place under grill and cook until golden and bubbling.

smoked salmon bites

ingredients

16 small pontiac potatoes
4 tablespoons vegetable oil
250 g (8 oz) smoked salmon
$^{1}/_{2}$ cup (125 ml, 4 fl oz) sour cream
3 hard-boiled eggs, cut into small wedges
fresh dill sprigs
makes 32

1 Preheat oven to 180°C (350°F, gas mark 4). Cut potatoes into thick slices and place in a large bowl. Add oil and toss to coat well. Place potato slices on baking trays and bake for 30 minutes or until tender. Remove potatoes from oven and cool slightly.

2 To serve, top each potato slice with a little salmon, a teaspoon of sour cream, an egg wedge and a dill sprig. Serve warm.

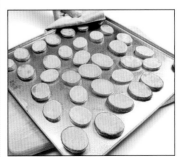

i

preparation time
10 minutes

cooking time
30 minutes

nutritional value per serve
fat: 7.6 g
carbohydrate: 9.3 g
protein: 5.6 g

lobster filo triangles

ingredients

8 sheets filo pastry
125 g (4 oz) butter, melted and cooled
lobster cream filling
I cooked lobster
3 tablespoons butter
6 spring onions (green onions), chopped
2 cloves garlic, crushed
1½ tablespoons plain flour
4 tablespoons white wine
4 tablespoons thick cream
pinch cayenne pepper
freshly ground black pepper
makes 32

i

preparation time
15 minutes

cooking time
15 minutes

nutritional value
per serve
fat: 17.8 g
carbohydrate: 7.8 g
protein: 11.6 g

1 To make filling, remove meat from lobster, chop finely and set aside. Melt 3 tablespoons butter in a saucepan over a medium heat. Add spring onions and garlic and cook, stirring, until onions are tender. Stir in flour and cook for 1 minute.

2 Remove pan from heat and whisk in wine and cream, a little at a time, until well blended. Season to taste with cayenne and black pepper, return to heat and cook, stirring constantly, until sauce boils and thickens. Reduce heat to low and simmer for 3 minutes. Remove from heat, stir in lobster meat and cool completely.

3 Preheat oven to 220°C (425°F, gas mark 7). Cut pastry sheets lengthwise into 5 cm strips. Working with one strip of pastry at a time, brush pastry with melted butter. Place a teaspoonful of the filling one end of strip, fold corner of pastry diagonally over filling, then continue folding diagonally up the strip to make a neat triangle.

4 Place triangles on a lightly greased baking tray, brush with butter and bake for 10–15 minutes or until golden.

spiced apricot meat balls

ingredients

140 g (4¹/₂ oz) diced dried apricots
2 tablespoons brandy
500 g (1 lb) beef mince
1 medium onion, finely chopped
1 slice white bread, crusts removed and
    soaked in 4 tablespoons water
¹/₂ teaspoon ground cinnamon
pinch ground nutmeg
1 teaspoon salt
¹/₂ teaspoon pepper
1 egg
¹/₂ cup (125 ml, 4 fl oz) oil for frying
apricot dipping sauce
90 g (3 oz) dried diced apricots
1 cup (250 ml, 8 fl oz) water
2 teaspoons sugar
2 teaspoons balsamic vinegar
1 teaspoon teriyaki sauce
1 teaspoon fresh ginger juice
makes 20-25

i

preparation time
25 minutes, plus
1 hour soaking
and 1¹/₂ hours
refrigeration

cooking time
30 minutes

nutritional value
fat: 10.9 g
carbohydrate: 9.5 g
protein: 7.9 g

1 Soak the diced apricots in the brandy for 1 hour. In a large bowl, place the mince, onion, bread, cinnamon, nutmeg, salt, pepper and egg. Using hands, knead mixture until thoroughly combined. Cover and refrigerate 1 hour.

2 Remove meatball mixture from refrigerator. Take a heaped teaspoon of mixture and roll into a ball with wet hands. Flatten slightly and press thumb in centre to form a deep depression. Place ¹/₄ teaspoon soaked apricots in centre and remould into a ball, covering the apricot. Place on a flat tray and continue to roll the remainder. Cover with plastic wrap and refrigerate at least 30 minutes.

3 For the dipping sauce: Place diced apricots and water in a small pan with any remaining brandy-soaked apricots. Bring to the boil, reduce heat and simmer 15 minutes or until very soft. Stir in sugar, vinegar, teriyaki sauce and simmer 2 minutes. Puree in a blender or food processor. Stir in the fresh ginger juice and set aside.

4 Heat oil in a large, heavy-based frying pan. Fry meatballs in 2-3 batches, rolling them around the pan to cook all over and keep their shape (about 4-5 minutes each batch).

5 Drain on kitchen paper. Place on a heated serving platter, with dipping sauce in the centre and toothpicks for serving.

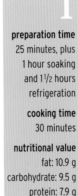

sweet

fruit tartlets

ingredients

pastry

185 g (6 oz) plain flour
2 tablespoons icing sugar
125 g (4 oz) butter
2 egg yolks
1 teaspoon water

custard cream filling

125 g (4 oz) sugar
6 teaspoons cornflour
2 eggs
1 egg yolk
3/4 cup (185 ml, 6 fl oz) milk
4 tablespoons thick cream
1 tablespoon orange-flavoured liqueur

tartlet filling

1 teaspoon gelatine
90 ml (3 fl oz) boiling water
155 g (5 oz) apricot jam, warmed
   and sieved
2 teaspoons orange-flavoured liqueur
440 g (14 oz) can apricot halves,
   drained and sliced
12 strawberries, halved or sliced
125 g (4 oz) seedless green or black
   grapes, halved
2 peaches, sliced
2 kiwifruit, sliced

makes 18

1 Preheat oven to 190°C (375°F, gas mark 5). To make pastry: In a food processor, place plain flour and icing sugar and process to combine. Add butter and process until mixture resembles fine breadcrumbs. With machine running, add egg yolks and water and process to form a rough dough. Turn dough out onto a lightly floured surface and knead until smooth. Wrap dough in plastic food wrap and refrigerate for 20 minutes.

2 Roll out dough to 3 mm thick. Using an 8 cm pastry cutter, cut out 18 rounds. Place pastry rounds in lightly greased patty pans (tartlet tins). Prick base and sides of pastry with a fork and bake for 10 minutes or until golden. Cool on a wire rack.

3 To make custard filling: In a bowl, place sugar, cornflour, eggs and egg yolk and whisk until smooth and thick. Heat milk and cream in a small pan over a medium heat, then gradually whisk in egg mixture. Reduce heat to low and cook, stirring constantly, until mixtures boils and thickens. Remove pan from heat, stir in liqueur, cover and set aside to cool.

4 To assemble: In a bowl, place gelatine and boiling water and stir until gelatine dissolves. Stir in jam and 2 teaspoons liqueur and set aside until glaze cools and begins to thicken. Spoon custard cream filling into pastry shells, then decorate with fruit and brush tops with gelatine mixture. Chill until firm.

i

preparation time
30 minutes,
plus 20 minutes
refrigeration

cooking time
10-20 minutes

**nutritional value
per serve**
fat: 7 g
carbohydrate: 21.7 g
protein: 2.6 g

For best results, chill pastry shells for 20 minutes before baking. Line shells with nonstick paper and fill with uncooked rice so the pastry does not puff during baking. Tartlet shells can be baked the day before, cooled completely and stored in an airtight container. To prevent the pastry from softening, it is best to fill, decorate and glaze fruit tartlets no more than 2 hours before serving.

orange and blueberry upside-down cakes

ingredients

orange and blueberry topping
2 small oranges, peeled
155 g (5 oz) fresh or frozen blueberries
1 tablespoon cornflour
1 tablespoon brown sugar
2 tablespoons sherry or brandy

almond cakes
115 g (4 oz) raw unsalted almonds,
    roasted and ground to a meal
90 g (3 oz) plain flour
1 teaspoon baking powder
4 egg whites
125 g (4 oz) sugar
2 egg yolks
1 teaspoon vanilla essence

orange custard (optional)
1 cup (250 g, 8 oz) low-fat custard
2 teaspoons orange blossom water,
    orange juice or orange flavoured
    liqueur
2 teaspoons grated orange rind (zest)
makes 12

1. In a jug, place custard, orange blossom water and orange rind. Mix to combine. Cover and refrigerate until ready to use.

2. In a large saucepan, place oranges and pour over water to cover. Bring to the boil. Reduce heat. Simmer for 10 minutes. Drain and set aside until cool enough to handle.

3. Preheat oven to 170°C (325°F, gas mark 3). Lightly spray or brush two nonstick 1-cup (250 ml, 8 fl oz) capacity muffin trays with unsaturated oil.

4. In a large bowl, place blueberries, cornflour, sugar and sherry. Toss to combine. Place an orange slice in the base of each muffin cup. Top with some of the blueberry mixture. Set aside.

5. For the cakes: Sift together ground almonds, flour and baking powder. In a large bowl, place egg whites and beat until soft peaks form. Gradually beat in sugar. Beat in egg yolks and vanilla essence. Continue beating until sugar dissolves.

6. Using a large spoon or spatula, fold in the flour mixture until just combined – take care not to over mix. Spoon batter into muffin cups. Bake for 15–20 minutes or until cooked when tested with a skewer. Stand muffins in tins for 5–10 minutes. Turn onto a wire rack. Serve warm with orange custard, if desired.

i

preparation time
20 minutes

cooking time
30 minutes

nutritional value per serve
fat: 4.7 g
carbohydrate: 30 g
protein: 3.7 g

macadamia and coffee marzipan

ingredients

270 g (9 oz) ground unsalted macadamias
100 g (3½ oz) pure icing sugar
100 g (3½ oz) castor sugar
6 teaspoons egg white (about 1 egg white)
1 tablespoon instant coffee dissolved in 1 tablespoon hot water
few drops vanilla essence
confectioner's rice paper
makes 36

4 To serve, remove greaseproof paper. Cut into 3 cm squares or desired shapes.

1 In a food processor, place ground macadamias, icing sugar and castor sugar. Process to combine. With machine running, slowly add egg white. Process until mixture just holds together.

2 Divide mixture in half and place in two bowls. Add coffee to one portion. Knead to combine. Add vanilla essence to the other portion. Knead to combine.

3 Line an 18 cm square shallow cake tin with rice paper. Press the coffee-flavoured mixture firmly into tin. Press vanilla-flavoured mixture on top. Cover lightly with greaseproof paper. Refrigerate overnight or until ready for use.

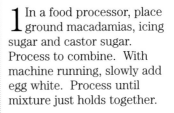

i

preparation time
20 minutes, plus overnight refrigeration

nutritional value per serve
fat: 4 g
carbohydrate: 16.4 g
protein: 6.8 g

snacks

1 In a large bowl, combine oil, lemon juice, onion and capers. Whisk to combine and set aside.

2 Arrange smoked salmon on serving plates.

3 Drizzle the dressing over the smoked salmon, sprinkle with parsley and ground black pepper, and serve. Garnish with extra capers.

smoked salmon carpaccio

ingredients

4 tablespoons extra virgin olive oil
45 ml (1¹/₂ fl oz) lemon juice
1 small red onion, finely chopped
2 teaspoons small whole capers
350 g (11¹/₂ oz) smoked salmon
1 tablespoon roughly chopped parsley
black pepper, freshly ground
extra capers for garnish
serves 4

i

preparation time
15 minutes

**nutritional value
per serve**
fat: 16.9 g
carbohydrate: 1.1 g
protein: 15.3 g

baked ricotta mushrooms

ingredients

10 large mushrooms, stems removed
1 tablespoon grated parmesan cheese
1 tablespoon dried breadcrumbs
ricotta and herb filling
125 g (4 oz) ricotta cheese
3 sun-dried tomatoes, soaked in warm
   water until soft, chopped
1 tablespoon finely diced red onion
1 tablespoon chopped fresh basil
1 tablespoon snipped fresh chives
1 teaspoon lemon juice
freshly ground black pepper
1 tablespoon brown sugar
makes 10

1 Preheat oven to 180°C (350°F, gas mark 4). Line a baking tray with nonstick baking paper. Set aside.

2 In a large bowl, place ricotta, tomatoes, onion, basil, chives, lemon juice and black pepper to taste. Mix to combine.

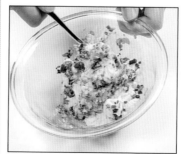

3 Spoon filling into mushroom caps and place on prepared baking tray. Combine parmesan and breadcrumbs. Sprinkle over mushrooms. Bake for 10–15 minutes or until filling is set and top is golden.

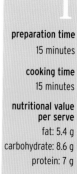

preparation time
15 minutes

cooking time
15 minutes

nutritional value per serve
fat: 5.4 g
carbohydrate: 8.6 g
protein: 7 g

roasted capsicum with feta and olives

ingredients

2 large red capsicums (peppers) halved
  and seeded
2 baby eggplants (aubergines), sliced
60 g (2 oz) semi sun-dried tomatoes
60 g (2 oz) olives
100 g (3¹/₂ oz) greek feta, cubed
2 tablespoons olive oil
2 teaspoons fresh oregano leaves
1 clove garlic, crushed
serves 4

1 Preheat oven to 180°C (350°F, gas mark 4).

2 Place capsicums on a lightly greased baking tray skin side down. Place eggplant slices, tomatoes, olives and feta inside capsicums.

3 In a jar, mix together olive oil, oregano and garlic. Drizzle this oil mixture over capsicums, and bake for 20–25 minutes.

i

preparation time
15 minutes,

cooking time
20-25 minutes

**nutritional value
per serve**
fat: 7.2 g
carbohydrate: 6 g
protein: 3.6 g

pork apple parcels

ingredients

800 g (1lb 10 oz) lean pork schnitzel, trimmed of fat, pounded until very thin
2 granny smith apples, chopped
60 g (2 oz) sultanas
juice of ½ lemon
½ cup (125 ml, 4 fl oz) plum sauce
½ cup (125 ml , 4 fl oz) apple juice
1 tablespoon soy sauce
1 tablespoon honey
makes 12 parcels

1 Preheat oven to 180°C (350°F, gas mark 4). Cut pork into 10 cm squares and set aside.

2 In a large bowl, place apples, sultanas and lemon juice. Mix to combine. Spread each pork square with plum sauce to within 2 cm of the edges, reserving 2 tablespoons plum sauce for dipping. Place a small mound of the apple mixture in the centre. Roll up to form a parcel. Tie with cooking string. Place in a lightly greased casserole dish.

3 Combine apple juice, soy sauce and honey. Pour over pork parcels. Cover loosely with foil. Bake for 20–25 minutes or until pork is browned and tender. Remove parcels from casserole dish and stir 2 tablespoons plum sauce into cooking juices. Serve with parcels for dipping.

i

preparation time
15 minutes

cooking time
25 minutes

nutritional value per serve
fat: 1.9 g
carbohydrate: 13.1 g
protein: 10.5 g

moroccan lemon chicken shish kebabs

ingredients

500 g (1 lb) chicken breast fillets,
  trimmed of fat, cut into 2 cm cubes
moroccan lemon marinade
1 tablespoon chopped parsley
1 tablespoon fresh rosemary leaves
2 teaspoons fresh thyme leaves
1 clove garlic, crushed
1 teaspoon black peppercorns, crushed
grated rind (zest) and juice of 1 lemon
1 tablespoon olive oil
8 large metal or bamboo skewers
makes 8 kebabs

i

preparation time
15 minutes, plus
30 minutes
marinating

cooking time
10 minutes

**nutritional value
per serve**
fat: 8.2 g
carbohydrate: 0.2 g
protein: 19.6 g

1 In a non-metallic bowl, place parsley, rosemary, thyme, garlic, black pepper, lemon juice and rind and oil. Add chicken. Toss to combine. Cover and refrigerate for at least 30 minutes.

2 Preheat barbecue or grill to a high heat. If using bamboo skewers, soak in cold water for at least 20 minutes.

3 Thread chicken onto skewers. Place on barbecue grill or under grill. Cook, brushing frequently with marinade and turning for 6–10 minutes or until chicken is cooked.

chicken and mushroom vol-au-vents

ingredients

75 g (2¹/₂ oz) butter
8 mushrooms, sliced
4 spring onions (green onions), sliced
1 tablespoon chopped fresh parsley
350 g (11¹/₂ oz) chicken breast fillets, diced
1 tablespoon plain flour
75 ml (2¹/₂ fl oz) carrot juice
1 tablespoon celery juice
1 tablespoon red capsicum (pepper) juice
100 ml (3¹/₂ fl oz) chicken stock
¹/₂ cup (125 ml, 4 fl oz) wine
salt and pepper
4 large vol-au-vent cases
makes 4 large vol-au-vents

i

preparation time
20 minutes

cooking time
35 minutes

nutritional value
per serve
fat: 8.8 g
carbohydrate: 3.1 g
protein: 8.5 g

1 Preheat oven to 190°C (375°F, gas mark 5). Heat 25 g (³/₄ oz) butter in a large frying pan and sauté mushrooms, spring onions and parsley on medium heat for 3–4 minutes. Remove from pan and set aside.

2 Add remaining butter and cook the chicken for 3–4 minutes until browned. Add flour, stir then add vegetable juices, stock, wine and salt and pepper. Bring to the boil, reduce heat, add mushroom mixture and stir through.

3 Fill vol-au-vent cases with chicken mixture and place on a lightly oiled baking tray in the oven for 15 minutes until heated through. Serve.

fried vongole

ingredients

2 eggs, lightly beaten
salt and pepper
200 g (7 oz) dry breadcrumbs
1 tablespoon dry mixed herbs
1 kg (2 lb) clams, cleaned and steamed
3 tablespoons tartare sauce
½ cup (125 ml, 4 fl oz) oil
serves 4

i

preparation time
15 minutes

cooking time
10 minutes

**nutritional value
per serve**
fat: 10.3 g
carbohydrate: 10.4 g
protein: 22.2 g

1 In a bowl, place eggs and season with a little salt and pepper. Combine breadcrumbs and herbs in a separate bowl.

2 Dip clams in egg mixture, then roll in breadcrumbs.

3 In a wok or a large frying pan, heat oil and deep fry clams in batches for 1–2 minutes until golden. Drain on absorbent paper and serve immediately with tartare sauce.

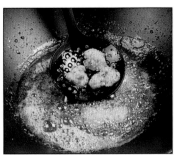

lobster crowns

ingredients

24 large mushrooms
$1/2$ teaspoon salt
dash pepper
2 tablespoons butter
extra 1 teaspoon butter
125 g (4 oz) lobster meat, diced
125 g (4 oz) cheddar cheese, grated
makes 24

1 Remove stems from mushrooms, finely dice stems and set aside. Season mushroom caps with salt and pepper. Heat a large frying pan with the 2 tablespoons butter over a medium heat. Fry mushrooms, tops down, for 2–3 minutes until browned.

2 Remove mushrooms from pan. In a small bowl, combine reserved diced stems, 1 teaspoon butter and lobster meat.

3 Preheat grill to high. Stuff mushroom caps with lobster mixture and sprinkle with grated cheese. Grill 4–5 minutes until golden.

i

preparation time
15 minutes

cooking time
10 minutes

nutritional value per serve
fat: 7.8 g
carbohydrate: 0.8 g
protein: 13.6 g

salmon vegetable parcels

ingredients

1 small orange sweet potato, sliced
lengthwise
1 large zucchini (courgette), sliced
lengthwise
1 large carrot, sliced lengthwise
4 large silverbeet or english spinach
leaves
4 x 150 g (5 oz) salmon or ocean trout
fillets, skinned and boned
1 teaspoon chopped fresh oregano
1 tablespoon chopped fresh parsley
crushed fresh black peppercorns
2-3 sprigs fresh oregano
2-3 large sprigs fresh parsley
water for steaming
serves 4

i

preparation time
25 minutes

cooking time
10 minutes

nutritional value
fat: 3.9 g
carbohydrate: 2.5 g
protein: 11.3 g

1 In a large pan of boiling water, cook sweet potato, zucchini and carrot until just tender. Drain well and set aside. Remove thick white stems from silverbeet. Gently boil or microwave spinach leaves until just wilted. Drain well and set aside.

2 Cut four pieces of plastic food wrap, each about 30 cm long. Place on work surface. Place a silverbeet leaf on each piece of food wrap and overlap edges where the stem has been removed. Place a piece of fish in the centre of each leaf. Sprinkle with oregano, parsley and black pepper.

3 Cover fish with sweet potato, zucchini and carrot slices. Wrap silverbeet around fish and vegetables to make parcels. Wrap plastic food

wrap around each parcel and tie ends in a knot to seal. Place on a plate. Cover and refrigerate until ready to cook.

4 In a wok, place oregano and parsley sprigs and 5 cm of water. Bring to simmering. Place fish parcels in a bamboo steamer and then place steamer over wok. Cover. Steam for 10 minutes or until fish just starts to flake when pressed with a fork – the cooked fish should still be pink inside.

5 To serve, remove plastic wrap, dispose of, and accompany fish parcels with steamed rice or potatoes and steamed vegetables of your choice.

marinated calamari with a lemon and herb dressing

ingredients

1 kg (2 lb) calamari (squid), cut into
  thin rings
90 ml (3 fl oz) lemon juice
3 cloves garlic, crushed
½ cup (125 ml, 4 fl oz) olive oil
dressing:
4 tablespoons lemon juice
90 ml (3 fl oz) olive oil
1½ tablespoons chopped fresh parsley
1 clove garlic, crushed
1 teaspoon dijon mustard
salt and pepper
serves 4-6

i

preparation time
10 minutes, plus
3 hours or
overnight
marinating

cooking time
5 minutes

**nutritional value
per serve**
fat: 10.1 g
carbohydrate: 0.3 g
protein: 13.5 g

1 In a large glass dish, place 90 ml (3 fl oz) lemon juice, 3 cloves garlic and ½ cup (125 ml, 4 fl oz) oil. Add calamari, cover and refrigerate for 3 hours or overnight.

2 For the dressing: Place all ingredients in a large bowl or jar and whisk well, until thickened.

3 Heat a large pan or wok over a high heat and cook calamari 2–3 minutes until just cooked. Serve calamari drizzled with dressing.

scallops baked with cured ham

ingredients

2 tablespoons olive oil
500 g (1 lb) scallops, in half shell
salt and freshly ground black pepper
1 small onion, finely chopped
1 clove garlic, crushed
60 g (2 oz) minced cured ham, such
   as proscuitto
3 tablespoons dry white wine
60 g (2 oz) breadcrumbs
1 tablespoon chopped parsley
1 teaspoon lemon juice
salt to taste
serves 2

1 Preheat oven to 200°C (400°C, gas mark 6). Heat 1 tablespoon oil in a large frying pan and sauté scallops over high heat for 1 minute. Divide the scallops among the shells and sprinkle with salt and pepper.

2 Add the onion and garlic and a little more oil, if necessary, to the frying pan. Cover and cook over low heat for 15 minutes. Add the ham and sauté for 1 minute. Stir in wine and let it cook off. Spoon mixture over scallops.

3 In a small bowl, combine the bread crumbs, parsley, lemon juice and remaining oil. Sprinkle over the scallops. Place shells on baking sheet and bake 10 minutes. If necessary, put under the grill to brown the top.

i

preparation time
15 minutes

cooking time
25 minutes

nutritional value
per serve
fat: 5.9 g
carbohydrate: 5.7 g
protein: 10.1 g

thai prawn cakes

ingredients

500 g (1 lb) uncooked peeled prawns,
   deveined
2 spring onions (green onions),
   chopped
1 teaspoon finely chopped lemon grass
2 kaffir lime or lemon myrtle leaves,
   soaked in boiling water for 15
      minutes, finely chopped (optional)
1 egg white
1 tablespoon fish sauce
1 tablespoon lime juice
1 teaspoon sweet chilli sauce or to taste
4 tablespoons fresh breadcrumbs
2 tablespoons chopped fresh mint
2 tablespoons chopped fresh coriander
coriander dipping sauce
2 tablespoons chopped fresh coriander
1 spring onion, finely chopped
1 clove garlic, crushed
1 teaspoon brown or palm sugar
4 tablespoons rice or sherry vinegar
2 teaspoons low-salt soy sauce
1/2 teaspoon fish sauce
1/2 teaspoon chilli sauce (optional)
**serves 4 as a main meal or 8 as a
starter**

i

preparation time
15-20 minutes

cooking time
5-8 minutes

nutritional value
fat: 6.3 g
carbohydrate: 4.4 g
protein: 14.5 g

1 Place prawns in a food processor. Using the pulse button, process until roughly chopped. Add spring onions, lemon grass, lime leaves, egg white, fish sauce, lime juice and chilli sauce. Using the pulse button, process until just combined. Transfer mixture to a large bowl. Fold in breadcrumbs, mint and coriander.

2 Shape mixture into 4 cm round patties. Place on a plate lined with plastic food wrap or thread 2–3 patties on a lemon grass skewer (see cook's tip below). Cover. Refrigerate for 30 minutes or until patties are firm.

3 Preheat a barbecue to a medium heat. Add patties. Cook for 2–3 minutes each side or until lightly browned.

Alternatively, heat a nonstick frying pan over a medium heat. Lightly spray or brush with unsaturated oil and pan-fry, or cook under a medium grill or bake in the oven at 200°C (400°F, gas mark 6) – if baking do not thread onto lemon grass skewers.

4 For the dipping sauce: Place coriander, spring onion, garlic, sugar, vinegar and fish, soy and chilli sauces in a bowl. Whisk to combine. Serve with prawn cakes for dipping.

cook's tip: Crab or white fish fillets can be used instead of prawns to make these fish cakes. For an attractive presentation and added flavour, thread prepared prawn cakes onto fresh lemon grass stems, then cook on the barbecue. Soak the lemon grass stems in cold water for 1 hour before using – this helps prevent the skewers from burning during cooking.

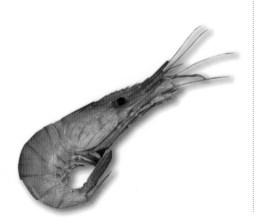

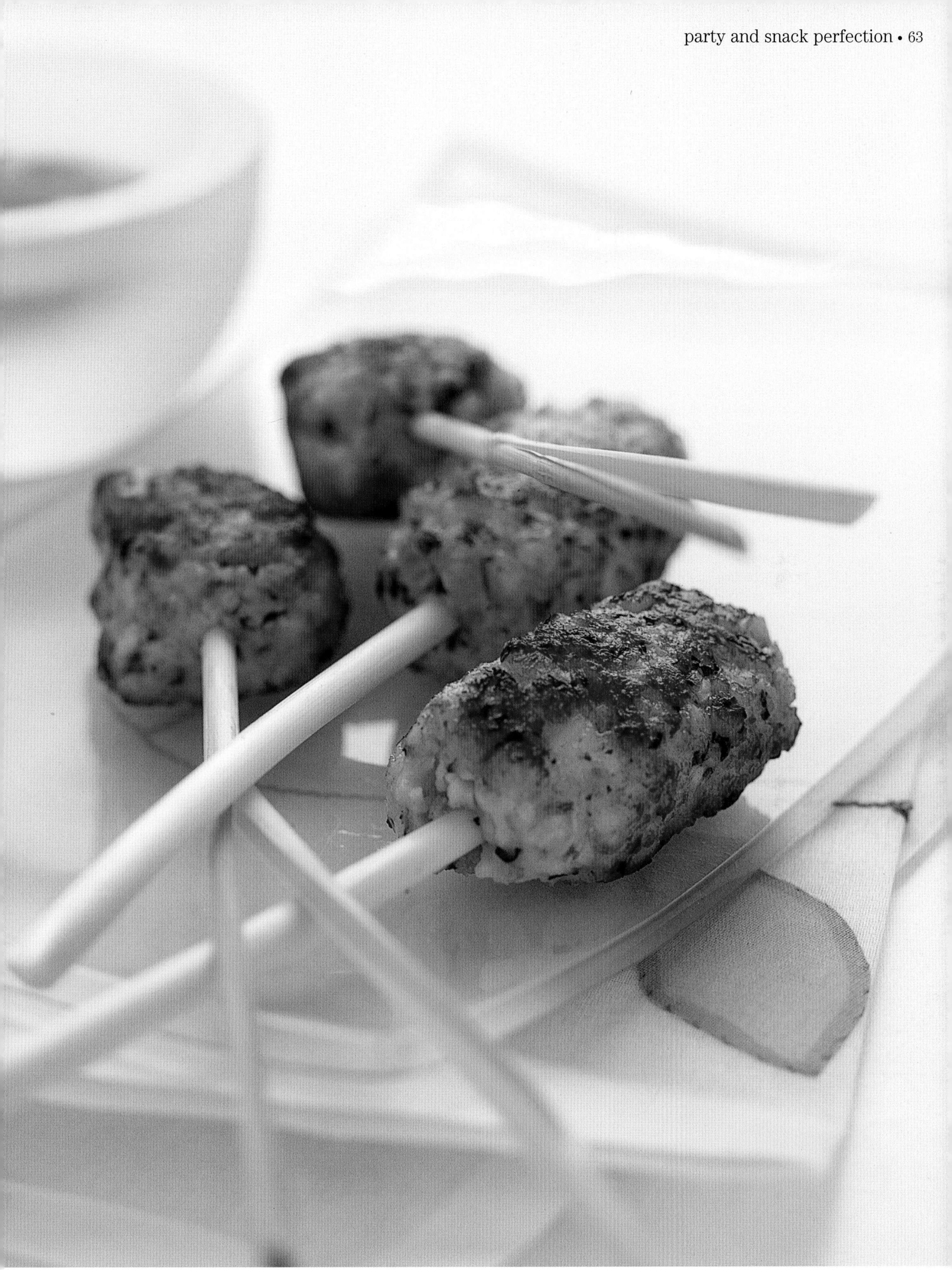

feta and ricotta stuffed tomatoes

ingredients

6 large firm tomatoes
150 g (5 oz) feta cheese, crumbed
150 g (5 oz) ricotta cheese
60 g (2 oz) pine nuts, chopped
10 black olives, pitted and chopped
1$\frac{1}{2}$ tablespoons chopped fresh oregano
3 tablespoons wholemeal breadcrumbs
freshly ground black pepper
6 black olives, to garnish
extra oregano leaves to garnish
serves 6

i

preparation time
15-20 minutes

cooking time
5-8 minutes

nutritional value
fat: 6.2 g
carbohydrate: 3.6 g
protein: 4.2 g

1 Preheat oven to 180°C (350°F, gas mark 4).

2 Cut a lid off the top of each tomato and set aside. Carefully scoop the centre of each tomato into a large bowl. Combine half the tomato mixture with the feta, ricotta, pine nuts, olives, oregano, breadcrumbs and pepper. Beat mixture together, and spoon back into the cases (piling the tops high). Discard left over tomato flesh.

3 Place in a lightly greased shallow oven-proof dish and bake for 20–25 minutes.

4 Garnish with an olive and oregano and serve.

sherried crabmeat

ingredients

2 tablespoons butter
290 g (9 oz) mushrooms
extra 3 tablespoons butter
3 tablespoons plain flour
1 cup (250 ml, 8 fl oz) chicken stock
$\frac{1}{2}$ cup (125 ml, 4 fl oz) cream
500 g (1 lb) crabmeat, flaked
60 g (2 oz) parmesan cheese
60 g (2 oz) baby spinach leaves
$\frac{1}{2}$ red capsicum (pepper), finely diced
salt and cracked black peppercorns
2 tablespoons dry sherry
12 small vol-au-vent cases

serves 4-6

i

preparation time
15 minutes

cooking time
10 minutes, plus
heating
vol-au-vents

**nutritional value
per serve**
fat: 11.1 g
carbohydrate: 4.8 g
protein: 7.1 g

1 Heat 2 tablespoons butter in a large frying pan and sauté mushrooms for 2–3 minutes until lightly browned. Set aside.

2 In a separate pan, melt extra butter. Add flour and cook, stirring, on low to medium heat for 2 minutes.

3 Stir in chicken stock and cream. When sauce is boiling, add crabmeat and mushrooms.

4 Bring sauce to boil and add parmesan, spinach, capsicum, salt and pepper. Remove from heat and add sherry. Heat vol-au-vents according to packet directions. Spoon filling into vol-au-vent cases.

apricot and sausage kebabs

1 Preheat grill to medium high. Prick sausages with a fork and cook for 8–10 minutes, turning frequently to cook evenly. Allow to cool.

2 Cut into 1 cm thick slices. Thread each piece onto a cocktail stick and place apricot half at each end.

3 Preheat grill to high or oven to 180°C (350°F, gas mark 4). In a small bowl, combine honey, soy sauce and water. Brush over each kebab, place under a grill until well glazed, or in oven for 10 minutes. Serve hot as finger food.

ingredients

4 pork sausages
125 g (4 oz) dried apricots
1 tablespoon honey
2 teaspoons soy sauce
1 teaspoon water
makes 16

i

preparation time
5 minutes

cooking time
20 minutes

nutritional value per serve
fat: 12.5 g
carbohydrate: 21.6 g
protein: 8.3 g

polenta and corn fritters

ingredients

1¹/₂ cups (375 ml, 12 fl oz) water
¹/₂ teaspoon salt
75 g (2¹/₂ oz) polenta
100 g (3¹/₂ oz) corn kernels
1 spring onion (green onion), finely sliced
1 tablespoon finely chopped parsley
1 clove garlic, crushed
45g (1¹/₂ oz) plain flour
¹/₂ teaspoon baking powder
1 egg, lightly beaten
pepper and salt, to taste
4 tablespoons olive oil, enough
  to cover base of pan
makes 16

---

i

preparation time
10 minutes

cooking Time
10-15 minutes

nutritional value
fat: 10.8 g
carbohydrate: 9.2 g
protein: 2.6 g

1 In a large pan bring water and salt to boil. Gradually add polenta, stirring continuously for 3–5 minutes or until polenta becomes thick and comes together like glue.

2 Remove from heat and add corn, spring onions, parsley and garlic. Stir until combined. Transfer to a bowl and set aside to cool.

3 In a bowl, sift together flour and baking powder. Add to polenta and mix to combine. Add egg, salt and pepper and mix to combine.

4 Heat oil in a large pan on a medium-high heat. Place tablespoons of polenta mixture in pan and cook in batches for 1–2 minutes on each side until lightly browned. Serve hot or cold. See below for pesto crème fraîche.

pesto crème fraîche

ingredients
3 tablespoons thickened cream
3 tablespoons sour cream
2 tablespoons pesto sauce
1 teaspoon lemon juice
salt and freshly ground black pepper,
  to taste
makes ³/₄ cup

1 Place all ingredients in a bowl and mix together, until smooth.

deep-fried okra

ingredients

250 g (8 oz) okra, washed and trimmed
1 egg
125 g (4 oz) plain flour
1 cup (250 ml, 8 fl oz) ice-cold water
oil, for frying

garlic walnut sauce
2 slices bread
²/₃ cup (170 ml, 5¹/₂ fl oz) water
60 g (2 oz) walnuts
2 cloves garlic, roughly chopped
2 tablespoons white-wine vinegar
1 tablespoon olive oil
salt and pepper
serves 4

i

preparation time
15 minutes

cooking time
10 minutes

nutritional value
fat: 8.1 g
carbohydrate: 11.7 g
protein: 4.1 g

1 For the garlic walnut sauce: In a small bowl, soak bread in water for 5 minutes, squeeze out water.

2 Place walnuts in a food processor, and process until finely chopped. Add bread, garlic and vinegar, and process until combined. While motor is running, add olive oil, salt and pepper, and process until paste is formed. Set aside until needed.

3 For the okra: In a large bowl, whisk egg until frothy. Add flour and water, and whisk until well combined and batter is frothy.

4 Heat the oil in a large frying pan. Dip okra in batter and cook in oil on a medium heat for 1–2 minutes or until lightly brown.

5 Drain on absorbent paper and serve with lemon wedges and garlic walnut sauce.

potato feta fritters

ingredients

245 g (7 ¹/₂ oz) potato, cooked
  and mashed
125 g (4 oz) feta cheese, crumbled
1 egg beaten
3 spring onions (green onions), chopped
3 tablespoons chopped fresh dill
1 tablespoon lemon juice
finely grated rind (zest) of ¹/₂ lemon
freshly ground black pepper
flour, for dredging
4 tablespoons olive oil
extra dill and lemon for garnish
serves 4

i

preparation time
10 minutes, plus
1-2 hours
refrigeration

cooking time
10 minutes

**nutritional value
per serve**
fat: 19.8 g
carbohydrate: 5.9 g
protein: 6.4 g

1 In a medium bowl, place the potato, feta, egg, spring onions, dill, lemon juice, rind and black pepper. Mix until well combined. Cover and refrigerate for 1–2 hours until firm.

2 Using hands, roll the mixture into golf ball-size fritters, and flatten slightly. Dredge lightly in flour, using a small sieve.

3 Heat olive oil in a large frying pan. Cook fritters in batches for about 3–5 minutes until golden brown on both sides. Drain on a paper towel and serve immediately. Garnish with extra dill and lemon.

roast pumpkin, potato and rosemary frittatas

ingredients

300 g (10 oz) butternut pumpkin, peeled, seeded and diced into 2 cm pieces

220 g (7$\frac{1}{2}$ oz) potatoes, peeled and diced into 2 cm pieces

220 g (7$\frac{1}{2}$ oz) sweet potatoes, peeled and diced into 2 cm pieces

1 tablespoon olive oil

2 sprigs rosemary, roughly chopped

$\frac{1}{2}$ teaspoon sea salt

4 eggs

$\frac{1}{2}$ cup (125 ml, 4 fl oz) cream

$\frac{1}{2}$ cup (125 ml, 4 fl oz) milk

1 clove garlic, crushed

60 g (2 oz) parmesan cheese, grated

salt and pepper to taste

serves 4

i

preparation time
15 minutes

cooking time
55 minutes

**nutritional value
per serve**
fat: 9.2 g
carbohydrate: 6.7 g
protein: 5.7 g

1 Preheat oven to 220°C (425°F, gas mark 7). Place pumpkin, potato, sweet potato, oil, half the rosemary and sea salt in a baking dish. Toss and bake for 20 minutes or until just cooked. Remove from oven and set aside.

2 Grease a 12 x 1 cup (250 ml, 8 fl oz) capacity muffin tin. Line bases with baking paper.

3 In a large bowl, combine eggs, cream, milk, garlic, parmesan, remaining rosemary and salt and pepper. Add potato, pumpkin and sweet potato. Reduce oven to 180°C (350°F, gas mark 4).

4 Pour mixture into muffin tins and bake for 30–35 minutes.

glossary

al dente: Italian term to describe pasta and rice that are cooked until tender but still firm to the bite.

bake blind: to bake pastry cases without their fillings. Line the raw pastry case with greaseproof paper and fill with raw rice or dried beans to prevent collapsed sides and puffed base. Remove paper and fill 5 minutes before completion of cooking time.

baste: to spoon hot cooking liquid over food at intervals during cooking to moisten and flavour it.

beat: to make a mixture smooth with rapid and regular motions using a spatula, wire whisk or electric mixer; to make a mixture light and smooth by enclosing air.

beurre manié: equal quantities of butter and flour mixed together to a smooth paste and stirred bit by bit into a soup, stew or sauce while on the heat to thicken. Stop adding when desired thickness results.

bind: to add egg or a thick sauce to hold ingredients together when cooked.

blanch: to plunge some foods into boiling water for less than a minute and immediately plunge into iced water. This is to brighten the colour of some vegetables; to remove skin from tomatoes and nuts.

blend: to mix 2 or more ingredients thoroughly together; do not confuse with blending in an electric blender.

boil: to cook in a liquid brought to boiling point and kept there.

boiling point: when bubbles rise continually and break over the entire surface of the liquid, reaching a temperature of 100°C (212°F). In some cases food is held at this high temperature for a few seconds then heat is turned to low for slower cooking. See simmer.

bouquet garni: a bundle of several herbs tied together with string for easy removal, placed into pots of stock, soups and stews for flavour. A few sprigs of fresh thyme, parsley and bay leaf are used. Can be purchased in sachet form for convenience.

caramelise: to heat sugar in a heavy-based pan until it liquefies and develops a caramel colour. Vegetables such as blanched carrots and sautéed onions may be sprinkled with sugar and caramelised.

chill: to place in the refrigerator or stir over ice until cold.

clarify: to make a liquid clear by removing sediments and impurities. To melt fat and remove any sediment.

coat: to dust or roll food items in flour to cover the surface before the food is cooked. Also, to coat in flour, egg and breadcrumbs.

cool: to stand at room temperature until some or all heat is removed, eg, cool a little, cool completely.

cream: to make creamy and fluffy by working the mixture with the back of a wooden spoon, usually refers to creaming butter and sugar or margarine. May also be creamed with an electric mixer.

croutons: small cubes of bread, toasted or fried, used as an addition to salads or as a garnish to soups and stews.

crudite: raw vegetable sticks served with a dipping sauce.

crumb: to coat foods in flour, egg and breadcrumbs to form a protective coating for foods which are fried. Also adds flavour, texture and enhances appearance.

cube: to cut into small pieces with six even sides, eg, cubes of meat.

cut in: to combine fat and flour using 2 knives scissor fashion or with a pastry blender, to make pastry.

deglaze: to dissolve dried out cooking juices left on the base and sides of a roasting dish or frying pan. Add a little water, wine or stock, scrape and stir over heat until dissolved. Resulting liquid is used to make a flavoursome gravy or added to a sauce or casserole.

degrease: to skim fat from the surface of cooking liquids, eg, stocks, soups, casseroles.

dice: to cut into small cubes.

dredge: to heavily coat with icing sugar, sugar, flour or cornflour.

dressing: a mixture added to completed dishes to add moisture and flavour, eg, salads, cooked vegetables.

drizzle: to pour in a fine thread-like stream moving over a surface.

egg wash: beaten egg with milk or water used to brush over pastry, bread dough or biscuits to give a sheen and golden brown colour.

essence: a strong flavouring liquid, usually made by distillation. Only a few drops are needed to flavour.

fillet: a piece of prime meat, fish or poultry which is boneless or has all bones removed.

flake: to separate cooked fish into flakes, removing any bones and skin, using 2 forks.

flame: to ignite warmed alcohol over food or to pour into a pan with food, ignite then serve.

flute: to make decorative indentations around the pastry rim before baking.

fold in: combining of a light, whisked or creamed mixture with other ingredients. Add a portion of the other ingredients at a time and mix using a gentle circular motion, over and under the mixture so that air will not be lost. Use a silver spoon or spatula.

glaze: to brush or coat food with a liquid that will give the finished product a glossy appearance, and on baked products, a golden brown colour.

grease: to rub the surface of a metal or heatproof dish with oil or fat, to prevent the food from sticking.

herbed butter: softened butter mixed with finely chopped fresh herbs and re-chilled. Used to serve on grilled meats and fish.

hors d'ouvre: small savoury foods served as an appetiser, popularly known today as 'finger food'.

infuse: to steep foods in a liquid until the liquid absorbs their flavour.

joint: to cut poultry and game into serving pieces by dividing at the joint.

julienne: to cut some food, eg, vegetables and processed meats into fine strips the length of matchsticks. Used for inclusion in salads or as a garnish to cooked dishes.

knead: to work a yeast dough in a pressing, stretching and folding motion with the heel of the hand until smooth and elastic to develop the gluten strands. Non-yeast doughs should be lightly and quickly handled as gluten development is not desired.

line: to cover the inside of a baking tin with paper for the easy removal of the cooked product from the baking tin.

macerate: to stand fruit in a syrup, liqueur or spirit to give added flavour.

marinade: a flavoured liquid, into which food is placed for some time to give it flavour and to tenderise. Marinades include an acid ingredient such as vinegar or wine, oil and seasonings.

mask: to evenly cover cooked food portions with a sauce, mayonnaise or savoury jelly.

pan-fry: to fry foods in a small amount of fat or oil, sufficient to coat the base of the pan.

parboil: to boil until partially cooked. The food is then finished by some other method.

pare: to peel the skin from vegetables and fruit. Peel is the popular term but pare is the name given to the knife used; paring knife.

pith: the white lining between the rind and flesh of oranges, grapefruit and lemons.

pit: to remove stones or seeds from olives, cherries, dates.

pitted: the olives, cherries, dates etc, with the stone removed, eg, purchase pitted dates.

poach: to simmer gently in enough hot liquid to almost cover the food so shape will be retained.

pound: to flatten meats with a meat mallet; to reduce to a paste or small particles with a mortar and pestle.

simmer: to cook in liquid just below boiling point at about 96°C (205°F) with small bubbles rising gently to the surface.

skim: to remove fat or froth from the surface of simmering food.

stock: the liquid produced when meat, poultry, fish or vegetables have been simmered in water to extract the flavour. Used as a base for soups, sauces, casseroles etc. Convenience stock products are available.

sweat: to cook sliced onions or vegetables, in a small amount of butter in a covered pan over low heat, to soften them and release flavour without colouring.

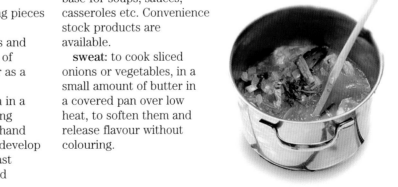

conversions

easurements differ from country to country, so it's important to understand what the differences are. This Measurements Guide gives you simple 'at-a-glance' information for using the recipes in this book, wherever you may be.

Cooking is not an exact science – minor variations in measurements won't make a difference to your cooking.

equipment

There is a difference in the size of measuring cups used internationally, but the difference is minimal (only 2–3 teaspoons). We use the Australian standard metric measurements in our recipes:

1 teaspoon ....5 ml   **1 tablespoon....20 ml**
½ cup......125 ml   **1 cup.....250 ml**
4 cups...1 litre

Measuring cups come in sets of one cup (250 ml), ½ cup (125 ml), ⅓ cup (80 ml) and ¼ cup (60 ml). Use these for measuring liquids and certain dry ingredients.
Measuring spoons come in a set of four and should be used for measuring dry and liquid ingredients.
When using cup or spoon measures always make them level (unless the recipe indicates otherwise).

dry versus wet ingredients

While this system of measures is consistent for liquids, it's more difficult to quantify dry ingredients. For instance, one level cup equals: 200 g of brown sugar; 210 g of castor sugar; and 110 g of icing sugar.

When measuring dry ingredients such as flour, don't push the flour down or shake it into the cup. It is best just to spoon the flour in until it reaches the desired amount. When measuring liquids use a clear vessel indicating metric levels.

Always use medium eggs (55–60 g) when eggs are required in a recipe.

dry

metric (grams)	imperial (ounces)
30 g	1 oz
60 g	2 oz
90 g	3 oz
100 g	3½ oz
125 g	4 oz
150 g	5 oz
185 g	6 oz
200 g	7 oz
250 g	8 oz
280 g	9 oz
315 g	10 oz
330 g	11 oz
370 g	12 oz
400 g	13 oz
440 g	14 oz
470 g	15 oz
500 g	16 oz (1 lb)
750 g	24 oz (1½ lb)
1000 g (1 kg)	32 oz (2 lb)

liquids

metric (millilitres)	imperial (fluid ounces)
30 ml	1 fl oz
60 ml	2 fl oz
90 ml	3 fl oz
100 ml	3½ fl oz
125 ml	4 fl oz
150 ml	5 fl oz
190 ml	6 fl oz
250 ml	8 fl oz
300 ml	10 fl oz
500 ml	16 fl oz
600 ml	20 fl oz (1 pint)*
1000 ml (1 litre)	32 fl oz

*Note: an American pint is 16 fl oz.

oven
Your oven should always be at the right temperature before placing the food in it to be cooked. Note that if your oven doesn't have a fan you may need to cook food for a little longer.

microwave
It is difficult to give an exact cooking time for microwave cooking. It is best to watch what you are cooking closely to monitor its progress.

standing time
Many foods continue to cook when you take them out of the oven or microwave. If a recipe states that the food needs to 'stand' after cooking, be sure not to overcook the dish.

can sizes

The can sizes available in your supermarket or grocery store may not be the same as specified in the recipe. Don't worry if there is a small variation in size—it's unlikely to make a difference to the end result.

cooking temperatures	°C (celsius)	°F (fahrenheit)	gas mark
very slow	120	250	½
slow	150	300	2
moderately slow	160	315	2-3
moderate	180	350	4
moderate hot	190	375	5
	200	400	6
hot	220	425	7
very hot	230	450	8
	240	475	9
	250	500	10

index